The Path to the Blossoms

By Spencer White

April put on a jacket and went to find her father.

“Dad, can we go and see the spring blossoms today?” asked April.

“Yes, but after I finish my coffee!” replied Dad.

“Okay, but drink it fast!” cried April, who was quite excited.

They would take their new tandem bike for a spin at last! It was red and had a brass basket on the back.

“You’ll be cold without a jacket, Dad,” said April.

April put on her helmet while her father grabbed a jacket.

"All set?" asked Dad.

“What about snacks?” April asked. “And a picnic rug for the grass?”

“You get a rug, and I’ll see what snacks we have,” Dad said.

I didn't know what you would rather eat, so I got tomato salad and last night's pasta. And I packed two flasks.

Dad got on the bike and grasped the front bar.

“Not so fast, Dad!” April said. “Where is your helmet?”

Dad put on his helmet.

April got on the bike behind him.

"All set, at last!" said April.

"Can we even ride this bike?"
Dad asked.

"Ha ha, yes!" said April.
"You push your pedals, and I push mine at the same time."

“We can do this,” said April.
“But let’s not go too fast!”

They rode off down the path.

Soon, they were riding past plum trees in bloom.

Dad gasped!

Let's have our snacks on the grass among the blossoms!

April grasped a bunch of blossoms in her hand.

"I'll take some blossoms home for my crafts!" said April.

She and Dad had a blast!

CHECKING FOR MEANING

1. What were April and Dad going to see? *(Literal)*
2. What snacks did April and Dad take to eat? *(Literal)*
3. Why do you think April suggested that they should not ride too fast? *(Inferential)*
4. Did Dad pick a good spot for their picnic? Why? *(Evaluative)*

EXTENDING VOCABULARY

spin	What does it mean to take a bike *for a spin*? Why do you think we use that phrase about bikes?
gasped	What is the base of the word *gasped*? What does someone do when they gasp? How might they feel?
blast	What does it mean that April and Dad *had a blast*? What is another way of saying that?

MOVING BEYOND THE TEXT

1. April reminded Dad to wear his helmet when riding their bike. What are some other ways people can be safe when riding bikes?
2. When it's cold, a jacket can help you stay warm. What other types of clothing can protect you from the cold?
3. What is your favourite season of the year? Why?
4. In the story, April and Dad had to work as a team to ride the tandem bike. When have you had to work as a team to do something?

TIME TO WRITE

Write about something you love that you can see or do during a particular season.